CIVIL WAR

Fast Facts About the Battle Between North and South

T. Robert Smithson

For Stella

CONTENTS

BACKGROUND

The American Civil War was the most significant and bloodiest conflict in North America.

It began on April 12, 1861 with the bombardment of Fort Sumter and ended on May 26, 1865, when General Buckner, acting for General Smith, surrendered the Army of the Trans-Mississippi.

More than a month earlier, General Robert Lee surrendered his Army of Northern Virginia at the Appomattox Courthouse.

At least 365,000 and 280,000 soldiers died in the Union and Confederate armies, respectively. Total civilian casualties were estimated at around 50,000.

Brother Vs. Brother

The Civil War split families, broke friendships, and tested loyalties as Americans had to fight against each other. Some people chose country over family and others chose the reverse.

Some wounds never healed, and some choices were never forgiven. Virginia-born Union General George Thomas died soon after the war, but his blood relatives didn't attend his funeral.

Others chose the other side because of their wife's influence. Among them was General John Pemberton who joined the Confederacy despite being born in Pennsylvania and having brothers fighting for the Union.

CAUSES

Slavery

Historians have put forth a variety of theories on the origins of the American Civil War, but it is generally accepted that slavery was its primary cause.

In the days leading to the civil war, the main political battle was whether slavery could expand into newly gained Western territories when they became states. When Lincoln, perceived to be anti-slavery, won the elections in 1860, several states acted and formed the Confederate States of America.

In turn, every state in the Confederacy issued an "Article of Secession," which explained why they were leaving the union.

Most explicitly stated their view that slavery should be retained and even expanded. One state called slavery "the greatest material interest in the world." It also declared, "We must either submit to degradation, and to the loss of property worth four billions of money, or we must secede from the Union framed by our fathers, to secure this as well as every other species of property."

Another declared that "the servitude of the African race, as existing in these States is mutually beneficial to both bond and free, and is abundantly authorized and justified by the experience of mankind, and the revealed will of the Almighty Creator, as recognized by all Christian nations."

Alexander Stephens, Vice President of the Confederacy later said that the Confederacy's cornerstone "rests upon the great truth, that the Negro is not equal to the white man; that slavery

—subordination to the superior race—is his natural and normal condition."

States' Rights

Another cause usually mentioned is States' Rights. The seceding states argued the union among the states was a compact and if they were not happy with what they received in return from, or with the policies of the federal government, they could end the relationship. The South felt that the Federal government did not honor the covenant enough and seceded.

One reason for the dissatisfaction was the Fugitive Slave Act of 1850, which mandated that fugitive slaves be returned to the South. The North hadn't enforced the law to the South's satisfaction. They allege that even slaves charged with alleged crimes but took refuge in the North were not returned to the South.

While most citizens in the South had none or few slaves, the rich dominated politics. The leaders sought to preserve the status quo, while for most ordinary soldiers the Civil War was a simple fight for their families and homes.

Other Causes

Other causes also usually mentioned were partisan politics, disagreements over tariffs, and dissatisfaction with federal military protection. The last one involved alleged inadequate federal protection from the Native Americans in nearby territories and the Mexican bandits who raided the state.

Later, an estimated 20,000 Native Americans joined the conflict and fought for both sides.

There was also a clandestine group of Americans, The Knights of the Golden Circle that worked to annex Mexico as part of the US.

LEGISLATION

When many Southern Democratic members left to join the Confederacy, Republicans dominated Congress. This enabled Lincoln and his allies to enact legislation that the Southern lawmakers opposed.

Among the most significant laws passed during this time were the Homestead Act, the Pacific Railway Act, and the Internal Revenue Act.

The Homestead Act provided free title to up to 160 acres of undeveloped federal land to anyone willing to live on and cultivate it.

The Pacific Railway Act allowed the building of a transcontinental railroad linking the Eastern and Western United States.

Finally, the Internal Revenue Act of 1861 taxed imports and imposed the first income tax in the US at 3% for incomes over $800 (about $27,000 in 2022 dollars).

STATES

South Carolina was the first state to secede on December 20, 1860. Within three weeks, Mississippi, Florida, and Alabama had followed suit.

Northern States

The Union included New York, Maine, Wisconsin, West Virginia, New Hampshire, Vermont, Massachusetts, Connecticut, Rhode Island, Pennsylvania, New Jersey, Ohio, Indiana, Illinois, Kansas, Michigan, Minnesota, Iowa, California, Nevada, and Oregon.

At the start of the war, the Union had a human resources advantage over the South of 5 to 2.

Southern States

The Confederacy included Virginia, Florida, Texas, Arkansas, Louisiana, Tennessee, Mississippi, Alabama, South Carolina, North Carolina and Georgia.

Tennessee was the last to secede on June 8,1861. It was also the first to be re-admitted to the Union after the war ended on July 24,1866. The last two to be readmitted were Texas on March 30,1870 and Georgia on July 15,1870. Georgia was supposed to rejoin the Union in July 1868 but it expelled some of its black state representatives.

Border States

The Border States were slave states that did not secede from the union. They were Maryland, Delaware, Missouri, and Kentucky. A fifth border state, West Virginia, was admitted to the union in 1863. Lincoln employed both military and diplomatic solutions to ensure that these remained in the Union during the war.

Kentucky and Missouri had two state governments, one Confederate and the other loyal to the Union, and both claiming to be the legitimate representative of the state. But the two Confederate state governments never had significant control.

New States

Two states joined the Union during the Civil War: West Virginia and Nevada. Since Nevada became a state in wartime, it got its nickname The Battle Born State.

FAMOUS BATTLES

Battle of Fort Sumter (April 12 to 13, 1861)

Although there were no casualties in the battle, the bombardment of Fort Sumter was the first military action of the American Civil War.

The battle led to widespread support on both sides for a military solution to the issue of secession.

First Battle of Bull Run/ the First Battle of Manassas (July 21, 1861)

This was considered the first major battle of the war and fought in Prince William County, Virginia. With 847 soldiers killed and over 2700 wounded, it was the largest battle in the United States at that point. By war's end, it wouldn't even be in the top ten.

This victory boosted Southern morale. In the Union, it erased illusions that the war would be swift and the South was no match to the Union's superiority in number and resources.

Battle of Fort Donelson (February 11 to 16, 1862)

The Battle of Fort Donelson was the first major Union victory in the Civil War. It resulted in the loss of Kentucky and opened the Cumberland River for the Union, which was key in invading the south.

After this victory, the Union promoted a relatively unknown commander to Major General. His name: Ulysses S. Grant. In this battle, he also got his nickname Unconditional Surrender Grant as over 12,000 Confederates surrendered.

Battle of Shiloh (April 6 to 7, 1862)

The battle took its name after a small church named Shiloh, which ironically meant peace. In the first day of battle, the Confederate Army surprised the Union Army and overran the latter's camp. After the Union retreat, Confederate General Beauregard reported victory to headquarters. But the following day, Ulysses Grant launched a counterattack and swept the confederates away from the field.

During the battle, Albert Sidney Johnston became the highest-ranking Confederate officer killed in the war.

Battle of Antietam/ Battle of Sharpsburg (September 17, 1862)

The Battle of Antietam was the single, bloodiest day in the American Civil War with 22,727 casualties, including 3,675 killed and over 17,000 wounded.

Robert Lee's Army of Northern Virginia faced George McClellan's Army of the Potomac.

Before the battle, McClellan got a copy of Lee's battle plans, describing how he divided his army. But McClellan hesitated as he thought the Confederates outnumbered him, though at the time he had more soldiers, 65,000 compared to Lee's 40,000.

Historians believe McClellan could've crushed Lee had he acted swiftly, especially since only A. P. Hill's forced march and arrival late in the battle saved Lee's army from being routed.

Battle of Chancellorsville (April 30 to May 6 1863)

This was one of Robert Lee's most famous victories and was fought in Spotsylvania County, Virginia. He faced General Joseph Hooker who outnumbered him two to one.

This battle was notable for the loss of one of the Confederacy's greatest generals, Stonewall Jackson. It's also the battle where the Union fielded its biggest army, 133,868 versus

Lee's 60,298.

The South won decisively, but at a cost. In terms of casualties as a percentage of total strength, the South suffered a greater loss with 22.06% casualties compared to the Union's 12.85%.

Siege of Vicksburg (May 18 to July 4, 1863)

Lincoln called Vicksburg the key and believed they could not win the war until they had the key in the Union's pocket.

When Union General Ulysses Grant forced the surrender of Confederate John Pemberton, it split the confederacy into two and the key was firmly in the Union's pocket. The Mississippi river was once more fully controlled by the Union Army.

The Battle of Gettysburg initially overshadowed Grant's victory, but has since been regarded as a major turning point of the Civil War.

The citizens of Vicksburg did not celebrate the Fourth of July until the following century.

Battle of Gettysburg (July 1 to 3, 1863)

The Battle of Gettysburg was probably the most famous battle of the Civil War. It was fought in and around the town of Gettysburg, Pennsylvania between General Lee and General George Meade.

It was the bloodiest battle of the Civil War with over 51,000 casualties on both sides.

Gettysburg was also notable as it's the first battle where a Union General outsmarted and outperformed Robert Lee.

Along with Vicksburg, the battle gave the strategic initiative to the Union. From that point onwards, the Confederacy fought a mostly defensive war.

Battle of Chickamauga (September 18 to 20, 1863)

The Battle of Chickamauga was the most significant Union defeat in the Western theater and after Gettysburg, was the second bloodiest battle of the war.

William Rosecrans of the Union Army fought against Braxton Bragg of the Confederacy in Georgia. Technically, Bragg won the battle as he drove Rosecrans off the field, but he failed in his primary objective—to restore Confederate control of East Tennessee.

Battle of Atlanta (July 22, 1864)

Union General William Tecumseh Sherman defeated Confederate General John Bell Hood in this battle fought in Georgia.

This victory ensured Lincoln's victory in the 1864 presidential elections.

Upon the city's capture six weeks later, Sherman ordered the burning of military facilities, but fire spread to buildings in the business district and some private residences.

While this gave Sherman notoriety in the South for generations, it's commonly noted as among the first examples of total war.

After leaving Atlanta, Sherman began his March to the Sea, culminating in the capture of Savannah on December 21.

Battle of Appomattox Station and Courthouse (April 9, 1865)

This battle resulted in Robert Lee surrendering the entire Army of Northern Virginia to Ulysses S. Grant. After Lee's surrender, the collapse of the Confederacy became inevitable.

Six days later, Abraham Lincoln was assassinated.

GENERALS

SOME FAMOUS UNION GENERALS

Robert Anderson

Robert Anderson was the commander of Fort Sumter when the Confederates bombarded the fort.

John Buford

John Buford arrived first in the Battle of Gettysburg, holding the high ground as he waited for reinforcements. He would later serve as the Army of the Potomac's Chief of Cavalry.

Ambrose Burnside

Ambrose Burnside commanded the Army of the Potomac. He commanded the Union Army during the loss in the Battle of Fredericksburg.

He would later be famous for his beard. The term sideburns was based on his name.

Joshua Lawrence Chamberlain

Joshua Chamberlain was a college professor and later Union General from Maine and is best known for his actions at the Battle of Gettysburg. He defended Little Round Top from several assaults and when they ran out of ammunition; he ordered a bayonet charge that saved the Union's far left flank. For his gallantry and leadership, he was awarded the Medal of Honor.

George Armstrong Custer

George Custer's 400 men helped prevent J. E. B. Stuart's cavalry from joining Lee during the third day of Gettysburg.

He died during the Battle of the Little Big Horn at 36.

Charles Henry Davis

Charles Henry Davis was commander of the Western Gunboat Flotilla that operated on the Western Rivers during the Civil War.

Abner Doubleday

After the death of General John Reynolds, Doubleday was briefly in command of the Union forces during the Battle of Gettysburg. His force of 9,500 men held on for several hours against 16,000 Confederate soldiers. He eventually retreated and relinquished command to more senior officers.

Doubleday later gained greater fame as having allegedly invented baseball in Cooperstown, New York. Despite no historical proof that he invented baseball, the sports' hall of fame museum is in Cooperstown.

David Farragut

David Farragut was the first Rear Admiral, Vice Admiral, and Admiral in the US Navy.

During the Battle of Mobile Bay, he uttered the famous quote: "Damn the torpedoes!"

Andrew Hull Foote

Andrew Hull Foote for his actions during the Union victories at the Battle of Forts Henry and Donelson.

James A. Garfield

James Garfield was a Major General in the Union Army.

In 1881, he became the 20th President of the United States. Six months into office, he was assassinated and died from his wounds. He was only 49.

David McMurtrie Gregg

David Gregg was a Major General and Cavalry Officer in the

Union Army. During the Battle of Gettysburg, he fought against Confederate Cavalryman J.E.B Stuart.

Henry Wager Halleck

Henry Halleck was a General-in-Chief of the Armies of the United States. In 1864, the Army promoted his former subordinate Ulysses Grant to General-in-Chief and Halleck became chief of staff.

He didn't rate high in field battlefield command, but was exceptional in logistics and supply chain management. His actions ensured the army was always adequately supplied.

Winfield Scott Hancock

Winfield Hancock was a Major General in the Union Army. His most famous engagement was the defense of Cemetery Ridge during the Battle of Gettysburg.

In 1880, he ran as the Democratic Party's candidate for President. He lost a close election to James Garfield.

Joseph Hooker

Joseph Hooker was a commander of the Army of the Potomac and is best known for his defeat at the Battle of Chancellorsville against Robert Lee.

Philip Kearny

Philip Kearny was a Major General in the Union and was killed in the Battle of Chantilly.

George B. McClellan

George McClellan commanded the Union Army during the loss at the Seven Days Battle and the strategic victory at the Battle of Antietam. Lincoln dismissed him as he failed to pursue Lee after Antietam.

In 1864, he ran against Abraham Lincoln in the Presidential elections. People expected him to win until Sherman's victory in Atlanta convinced the public that the North could win the war.

James B. McPherson

James McPherson was a Major General killed during the Battle of Atlanta.

He was the second-highest ranking Union officer killed in action during the war. He was 35.

George Meade

History remembers George Meade for decisively defeating Robert Lee during the Battle of Gettysburg, despite assuming command just three days earlier.

He organized the Union defense during the battle, using interior lines to reinforce threatened sectors.

He was the longest-tenured commander of the Army of the Potomac, from 1863 to 1865.

Wesley Merritt

He was a cavalry commander during the Battle of Gettysburg.

He later took part in the Spanish-American war and was the first American governor-general of the Philippines.

John Pope

John Pope is best known for leading the defeated Union during the Second Battle of Bull Run.

David Dixon Porter

David Dixon Porter was the second man to attain the rank of Admiral. He played a major role in the Vicksburg campaign.

He was also known for being in The PeaceMakers painting, which depicted the only three-way meeting among Generals Grant and Sherman, and President Lincoln.

John F. Reynolds

John Reynolds was a Major General considered to be among the best generals in the war. During the Battle of Gettysburg, he reinforced John Buford and was killed just as the battle escalated.

Reynolds was 42.

William Rosecrans

Rosecrans was the Union Commander of the Army of the Cumberland. He led the Union during the disaster at Chickamauga, the most significant Union defeat in the Western Theater.

John Schofield

John Schofield was a recipient of the Medal of Honor who rose to the rank of Lieutenant General and Commanding General of the US Army.

He played a key role in the Battles of Franklin and Nashville.

Winfield Scott

Winfield Scott fought in the War of 1812, the Indian Wars, the Mexican War, and the American Civil War. Scott holds the record for the greatest length of active service as general in the U.S. Army.

He crafted the Anaconda Plan, which blockaded the Southern ports.

Due to advancing age and the Union's defeat at the First Battle of Bull Run, he resigned in October 1861.

John Sedgwick

John Sedgwick was the highest-ranking Union general to be killed in action during the War. He was killed during the Battle of Spotsylvania Court House in 1864.

He is remembered for his ironic last words, just before a sharpshooter's bullet killed him: "They couldn't hit an elephant at this distance."

Philip Sheridan

Philip Sheridan was one of the Union's primary Cavalry commanders. He later rose to become General of the Army.

After the war, Sheridan was credited for saving Yellowstone National Park.

William Tecumseh Sherman

William Tecumseh Sherman was among the best-known and most successful generals of the Union Army during the Civil War.

He was best known for the March to the Sea and his scorched earth policies.

During the Battle of Shiloh, his failure to deploy pickets ensured surprise for the Confederates. This almost cost the Union the battle, but he rallied the Army and held a defensive line.

Sherman grew notoriety in the South for the March to the Sea and the Carolinas campaign. He singled out South Carolina, the first state to secede from the Union. Under his command, his Army burned Columbia, the state capital.

The US' most famous tank of World War 2, the M4 Sherman, was named after him.

Daniel Sickles

Daniel Sickles was a Union General who lost his leg during the Battle of Gettysburg. During the battle, he advanced at the Peach Orchard without orders, and created a vulnerable salient. As expected, the Confederates focused on his Army and only Meade's clever use of interior lines prevented disaster.

After the battle, he ran a vicious campaign against General Meade's character.

Henry W. Slocum

Henry Slocum was a Union General who fought in most

major battles of the war from First Bull Run to Sherman's March to the Sea.

Like many Civil War generals, he joined politics after the war. He was a member of the House of Representatives, representing the 3rd District of New York.

George Henry Thomas

George Thomas was a Major General, born in Virginia, but remained in the Union Army. As a result, when he died in 1870, none of his blood relatives attended his funeral, never forgiving him for his loyalty to the Union.

He became famous for his actions at Chickamauga, earning the nickname of "The Rock of Chickamauga" for his stubborn defense. He later replaced William Rosecrans as Commander of the Army of the Cumberland.

At West Point, he was roommates with William Sherman. He finished 12th in a class of 42.

Lew Wallace

Lew Wallace was a Union Major General in the Army of the Tennessee. He took part in several major battles including Fort Donelson, Shiloh and Corinth. He was part of the military commission for the trials of the Lincoln Assassination. Wallace also presided over the trial of Henry Wirz, the Confederate commandant of the notorious Anderson prison camp.

He is best known as the best-selling author of Ben-Hur: A Tale of the Christ, published in 1880.

John Lorimer Worden

John Lorimer Worden was commander of the USS Monitor, the US Navy's first ironclad warship.

SOME FAMOUS CONFEDERATE GENERALS

P.G.T. Beauregard

P. G. T. Beauregard was a general responsible for some of the Confederacy's early successes, including the Battles of Fort Sumter and First Bull Run.

He created the initial designs of the Confederate Battle Flag.

Braxton Bragg

General Braxton Bragg was best known as the commander of the Army of Mississippi.

Although he won in the Battle of Chickamauga, most of the battles he took part in were major defeats for the Confederacy.

Franklin Buchanan

Franklin Buchanan was the only full admiral in the Confederate Navy during the Civil War. He commanded the ironclad CSS Virginia (formerly USS Merrimack).

Buchanan was wounded and captured during the Battle of Mobile Bay in 1864.

Simon Bolivar Buckner, Sr.

Simon Bolivar Buckner Sr. was a Lieutenant General in the Confederate Army.

Before the war, he helped a broke Ulysses S. Grant by covering his expenses. When he surrendered Fort Donelson to Grant, he expected generous terms from his old friend. Despite Grant's warm reception for his friend, he demanded and got Unconditional Surrender from Buckner.

He would later be Governor of Kentucky and a pallbearer during Grant's funeral.

Jubal Anderson Early

Early was a Confederate general best known for promoting the Lost Cause after the war.

Richard S. Ewell

Ewell was a Confederate General best known for his role in the Battle of Gettysburg. Lee ordered Ewell to take Cemetery Hill "if practicable." He disagreed and did not attack as he felt his troops were too tired. Historians have noted that had he attacked, the Confederates would've won the battle.

Nathan Bedford Forrest

Nathan Bedford Forrest was nicknamed "The Wizard of the Saddle" for his innovative cavalry tactics during the Civil War.

He was also the first Grand Wizard of the Ku Klux Klan.

Ambrose Powell Hill

Ambrose Powell Hill, better known as A. P. Hill was one of the Confederacy's most competent commanders. During the Battle of Antietam, he force-marched his army and arrived in time to save Lee's battered troops. Hill's arrival prevented a rout.

He was killed during the third Battle of Petersburg.

John Bell Hood

John Bell Hood was one of the South's most aggressive commanders. He was soundly defeated at the Battles of Franklin and Nashville, and after losing almost two-thirds of his men, the

Army of Tennessee ceased to be an effective fighting force.

Thomas J. "Stonewall" Jackson

Stonewall Jackson was Robert Lee's most famous subordinate. He distinguished himself in the major battles early in the war. Historians believed Lee would've won the Battle of Gettysburg had Jackson been with him instead of A. P. Hill.

He was killed by friendly fire during the Battle of Chancellorsville.

Albert Sidney Johnston

Unlike most Confederate commanders, Johnston was already a General when he joined the Confederacy. Until the rise of Robert Lee, he was considered the South's most able commander.

At Antietam, he became the highest-ranking Confederate officer killed during the war. He bled to death when he was shot in the leg and the blood got trapped in his long boots. It took a while for doctors to find the wound.

Joseph E. Johnston

Joseph Johnston was in the same West Point Class as Robert Lee, where he finished 13th out of 46th. Lee finished second.

He was part of most major battles during the war, winning most of his early campaigns. But he was roundly criticized for failing to aid General Pemberton and break the Siege of Vicksburg.

He died of pneumonia, ten days after attending Union General Sherman's funeral in the pouring rain.

Catesby ap Roger Jones

Catesby ap Roger Jones took part in the historic first battle between two ironclads. During the Battle of Hampton Roads he engaged the USS Monitor. The battle ended in a draw.

James Longstreet

James Longstreet was one of the foremost Generals of the

war. Lee called him his "Old War Horse."

His actions during the Battles of Second Bull Run and Chickamauga led to decisive Confederate victories.

During the Battle of Gettysburg, he openly disagreed with Lee's tactics including the infamous Pickett's Charge. This was a major reason he became a key villain among proponents of the Lost Cause.

John C. Pemberton

John Pemberton was the commanding general who surrendered Vicksburg to Ulysses S. Grant.

George Pickett

George Pickett was best known for the charge that bore his name, Pickett's Charge. Despite the defeat, some considered it "the high water mark of the confederacy."

Pickett finished 59th in a class of 59 at West Point.

Leonidas Polk

Leonidas Polk was known as "Sewanee's Fighting Bishop," having been a bishop of the Episcopal Church before becoming a Major General in the Confederate Army.

He was killed by artillery during the Atlanta Campaign.

J.E.B. Stuart

James Earl Brown Stuart was one of the War's most talented Cavalry commanders and was Robert Lee's trusted eyes. However, at Gettysburg his long absence denied Lee of crucial intelligence during the battle.

He died at the Battle of Yellow Tavern in 1864. He was 31.

GRANT VS. LEE

Ulysses S. Grant and Robert E. Lee were the two primary generals of the war, leading the Union and the Confederacy, respectively.

Their head-to-head battles decided the outcome of the Civil War.

ROBERT EDWARD LEE

Robert E. Lee was the overall commander of the Confederate States Army during the American Civil War. Until George Meade defeated him in the Battle of Gettysburg in 1863, he consistently won against Union armies even when his forces were significantly smaller.

His aggressive tactics led to spectacular victories, but also a high rate of casualty.

He is one of the greatest American combat commanders in history.

West Point

Lee famously did not receive any demerits during his stay at the Academy. Still, he finished second in his class, behind Charles Mason. Mason's and Lee's graduation point scores are still the highest in the history of West Point.

After graduation, he was commissioned a brevet second lieutenant in the Corp of Engineers. And in 1852, Lee was appointed superintendent of West Point.

Civil War

Lee refused an offer to be a Major General in the Union, choosing instead to join the Confederacy. While opposed to secession, he remained loyal to his native state, Virginia.

He first gained fame as a commander when, despite being outnumbered, he defeated George McClellan in the Seven Days Battles. He would soundly beat McClellan's two successors, Ambrose Burnside and Joseph Hooker.

Lee and the Army of Northern Virginia were confident when they invaded the North to force Lincoln to negotiate for truce and peace. But General Meade, recently appointed head of the Army of the Potomac, defeated Lee. His army never fully recovered from the setback.

In 1864, when Ulysses S. Grant launched his Overland Campaign and later the Siege of Petersburg, the Union's superiority in materiel and men came to bear. Unlike Lee's previous experiences with the other Union commanders he defeated, Grant did not retreat after a setback. His masterful maneuvers and numerical advantage pinned down Lee.

General Lee surrendered to General Grant after the Battle of the Appomattox Courthouse. This effectively ended the Civil War.

Arlington National Cemetery

Arlington National Cemetery is a 639-acre cemetery across the Potomac River. Robert Lee and his wife Mary Anna Custis Lee originally owned the estate. It became a national military cemetery.

ULYSSES S. GRANT

Ulysses S. Grant was Commander-in-Chief of the Union Army during the American Civil War. He was elected President of the US in 1869 and again in 1873.

The S in Ulysses S. Grant does not stand for anything and results from an error in his nomination to WestPoint. Grant eventually accepted the phantom middle name as his own, though his original full name was Hiram Ulysses Grant.

His campaigns and strategies continue to be studied in West Point to this day.

West Point

He entered West Point in 1839 where he got the nickname of U. S. Grant or Sam for "Uncle Sam." He finished 21st in a class of 39 and was commissioned a brevet second lieutenant.

In 1854, Grant resigned his commission, mainly because of alcohol. When he joined civilian life, he tried several careers including a bill collector and a farmer. At one point, he resorted to selling firewood on street corners where some of his former colleagues in the military recognized and him, shocked at how far he had fallen. Finally, broke and desperate, he returned home and joined his father's leather business as a clerk.

Civil War

Grant won the first major Union victory of the Civil War with his capture of Fort Donelson. His conquest of Vicksburg established him as the premier Union commander in the Civil War.

After the Civil War, he vehemently opposed efforts by Andrew Johnson to prosecute Lee and other Confederate generals with treason. Faced with the popular Grant's resignation as head of the army, Johnson dropped the cases.

In 1869, he succeeded Johnson as President.

When Grant died in 1885, among his pallbearers were Union generals Sherman and Sheridan, along with Confederate generals Buckner and Johnston.

Grant Vs. Lee By the Numbers

The North had to invade and conquer the South to win, while the South only had to hold on long enough for peace negotiations to happen, either with a new administration or from public pressure.

This meant the North had to conduct an aggressive offense, which in war in the period usually meant the potential for more losses.

Thus Grant had more casualties compared to Lee. Unlike Lee, however, he could easily replace these losses. This battle of attrition ultimately resulted in Lee's defeat.

This section shows the statistics from head-to-head battles between Grant and Lee. To establish greater context, there is a comparison of how they performed versus different generals in other famous battles.

Casualties include killed, wounded, missing, captured. Percentages are casualties relative to strength. Note that figures may differ slightly depending on the source.

Grant Vs. Other Generals

Shiloh (April 6 to 7, 1862)

Grant had 66,812 men vs. Albert Sidney Johnston's 61,025. Grant's casualty was 13,047 compared to Johnston's 10,699. Grant's casualty rate was 19.53% vs. Johnston's 23.94%.

Result: Union victory.

Champion Hill, part of Vicksburg Campaign (May 16,1863)*

Grant had 32,000 men vs. John Pemberton's 22,000. Grant's casualty was 2,457 compared to Pemberton's 3,840. Grant's casualty rate was 7.68% vs. Pemberton's 17.45%

Result: Union victory.

**In the resulting siege of Vicksburg, Pemberton surrendered 29,945 men.*

Lee Vs. Other Generals

Chancellorsville (May 1 to 4, 1863)

Joseph Hooker had 133,868 men vs. Lee's 60,298. Hooker's casualty was 17,197 compared to Lee's 13,303. Hooker's casualty rate was 12.85% vs. Lee's 22.06%

Result: Confederate victory.

Antietam/Sharpsburg (September 17,1862) *

George McClellan had 75,500 men vs. Lee's 52,000. McClellan's casualty was 12,401 compared to Lee's 10,316. McClellan's casualty rate was 16.43% vs. Lee's 27.15%.

Result: Union victory.

**Other sources put McClellan's number at 87,164 while Lee's is consistent at 38,000 to 40,000. This lowers McClellan's casualty rate to 14.23%.*

Gettysburg (September 17,1862)

George Meade had 93,921 men vs. Lee's 71,699. Meade's casualty was 23,049 compared to Lee's 28,063. Meade's casualty rate was 24.54% vs. Lee's 39.14%.

Result: Union victory.

FOUR BLOODIEST BATTLES BETWEEN GRANT AND LEE

Here are four the bloodiest battles that the two generals fought against each other.

The Wilderness (May 4 to 7, 1864)

Grant had 101,895 men vs. Lee's 61,025. Grant's casualty was 17,666 compared to Lee's 11,033. Grant's casualty rate was 17.34% vs. Lee's 18.08%

Result: Union victory.

Spotsylvania Courthouse (May 8 to 21, 1864)

Grant had 100,000 men vs. Lee's 52,000. Grant's casualty was 18,399 compared to Lee's 12,687. Grant's casualty rate was 18.4% vs. Lee's 10.53%

Result: Inconclusive.

Cold Harbor (May 31 to June 12, 1864)

Grant had 108,000 men vs. Lee's 59,000. Grant's casualty was 12,737 compared to Lee's 4,595. Grant's casualty rate was 11.79% vs. Lee's 7.79%

Result: Confederate victory.

Second Battle of Petersburg (June 15 to 18, 1864)

Grant had 62,000 men vs. Lee's 38,000. Grant's casualty

was 11,386 compared to Lee's 4,000. Grant's casualty rate was 18.36% vs. Lee's 10.53%

Result: Inconclusive

Here are the combined statistics for these four battles:

Grant had 371,985 men vs. Lee's 210,025. Grant's casualty was 60,188 compared to Lee's 32,315. Grant's casualty rate was 16.18% vs. Lee's 15.39%.

ARMIES

This section lists some of the major armies that fought in the Civil War.

CONFEDERATE ARMIES

The Army of Northern Virginia

The Army of Northern Virginia was a unit famously commanded by Robert Lee. The army delivered some of the Confederacy's greatest victories, including the Peninsula and Northern Virginia campaigns.

It had 92,000 soldiers at its peak in 1862. At Gettysburg in 1863, it had 75,000. At the start of the Appomattox campaign, it had 50,000. By the time Lee surrendered, casualties and desertion had reduced the Army to 28,000.

Army of Mississippi

Also known as the Army of the West and fought at Shiloh and Corinth. In late 1862, it was renamed Army of Tennessee.

Another version was called The Army of Vicksburg under General Pemberton. It ceased to exist when Pemberton surrendered Vicksburg.

Army of Tennessee

This was formed in 1862. It fought in the Battle of Stones River in January 1863 until the end of the war in 1865. Among its notable commanders were Braxton Bragg, Joseph Johnston, and John Bell Hood.

Army of the Trans-Mississippi

The army consisted mainly of soldiers from Texas, Louisiana, Arkansas, the Indian Territory (Oklahoma), and Confederate Arizona.

It was the last major Confederate Army to surrender during

T. ROBERT SMITHSON

the war.

SOME FAMOUS UNITS OF THE CONFEDERATE ARMY

Texas Brigade

The Texas Brigade, also known as Hood's Brigade was an elite infantry unit of the Confederate Army. It fought on almost every major battle on the Eastern Theater.

Stonewall Brigade

The Stonewall Brigade was one of the South's elite troops. It was trained and first led by General Stonewall Jackson. His training transformed even raw recruits into formidable soldiers.

At Spotsylvania Court House, all but 200 men became casualties.

Alabama 26th Infantry Regiment

The Alabama 26th was composed of ten companies that came from various parts of Alabama. It served in both the Army of Northern Virginia and the Army of Tennessee.

26th North Carolina Regiment

The 26th North Carolina was composed of ten companies from North Carolina and Virginia.

It is the regiment with the largest number of casualties on either side during the war.

UNION ARMIES

The Army of the Potomac

The Army of the Potomac was the Union's most famous military unit and fought mainly in the war's Eastern Theater. It fought in some of the war's most famous battles including Gettysburg, Antietam, First Bull Run, and the Appomattox campaign.

Among its notable commanders were George Meade, George McClellan, Ambrose Burnside, and Joseph Hooker.

Army of the Tennessee

Like the Army of the Potomac, it was present in most of the major battles of the Civil war including Shiloh, Vicksburg, the Atlanta Campaign and the March to the Sea.

Among its notable commanders were Ulysses Grant, William Sherman, James McPherson, and Joseph Hooker.

Army of the Cumberland

Formerly known as the Army of the Ohio, it fought mainly in the Western theater of the Civil War. It fought in the Battle of Chickamauga, which resulted William Rosecrans' departure.

Among the notable commanders were Generals Rosecrans and George Thomas.

Army of the Ohio

There were two armies named Army of the Ohio. The first became the Army of the Cumberland, while the second later became part of Sherman's army.

Among the notable commanders were Rosecrans, Don

Carlos Buell, Ambrose Burnside, and John Schofield.

SOME FAMOUS UNITS OF THE UNION ARMY

Irish Brigade

The Irish Brigade was part of the Union Army and consisted predominantly of Irish Americans. The brigade was famous for their war cry, the "Faugh a Ballaugh", which is an Anglicization of the Irish phrase, fág an bealach, meaning, "clear the way."

In the early days of the war, the Irish Brigade distinguished itself from the rest of the Army of the Potomac with its choice of weapon. They used the obsolete Model 1842 smoothbore muskets because of the deadly buck-and-ball shot which produced a shotgun effect in close-range combat.

Iron Brigade

The Iron Brigade was an elite unit in the Union Army, composed of soldiers from the Midwest. The unit had a reputation for discipline and tenacity.

It suffered the highest percentage of casualties in the war.

54th Massachusetts

The 54th Massachusetts was the second African-American regiment of the Union Army. It was formed soon after the Emancipation Proclamation.

Its gallantry during the assault on Fort Wagner became legendary.

Maine Volunteer Regiment

The 20th Maine Regiment became famous for its successful defense of Little Round Top during the Battle of Gettysburg.

GETTYSBURG

Gettysburg was the best-known battle of the war. It was also the bloodiest. This section discusses some of the major incidents and personalities in the battle.

Lee invades

In June 1863, Robert Lee's Army of Northern Virginia was in high spirits. Despite being outnumbered, they had just decisively defeated the Union at the Battle of Chancellorsville.

The Army of Northern Virginia and many officers in the Union Army believed Lee was invincible.

Lee hoped that a successful intrusion to the North would send the populace in panic and demand peace talks.

Initial Contact

Major General Henry Heth sent Brigadier General J. Johnston Pettigrew to search for supplies, mainly shoes. He expected little resistance except for probably the local militia. But Pettigrew was surprised to see Union General John Buford arriving and preparing a defense. He was unsure if Buford was just an isolated unit or part of a larger force. The Confederates returned with a huge reconnaissance party to determine the size and quality of the opposition.

Buford prepared to meet the approaching Confederates by occupying three ridges—Herr Ridge, McPherson Ridge, and Seminary Ridge. He hoped to delay them long enough to allow the reinforcements to occupy the strong defensive positions behind him at Cemetery Hill, Cemetery Ridge, and Culp's Hill.

The Battle of Gettysburg had begun.

Reynolds

John Reynolds, one of the North's most respected generals, was the first to arrive and reinforce Buford. As he urged a Wisconsin regiment onwards, however, he was shot in the neck and killed instantly.

As the battle raged, more soldiers from both Union and Confederacy arrive in the confusion.

Towards the end of the day, the Confederates had overwhelmed the Union army. They federals retreated to Cemetery Hill where General Otis Howard left a reserve brigade with infantry and artillery.

Hancock

General Winfield Hancock arrived to assess the situation. There was an initial confusion, as General Howard believed he was in command. He eventually followed General Meade's written orders and gave way to Wincock. Wincock agreed with Howard that they had a strong defensive position. As evening progressed, more and more units arrived and the Union position resembled a giant fishhook.

"Take the hill if practicable."

In probably the most famous, but unclear order of the war, General Lee ordered General Richard Ewell to take the hill if practicable. Given his exhausted troops, Ewell decided it was not practicable.

This became the biggest "what-if" in the battle.

Fishhook

As evening progressed, more units arrived and the Union position resembled a giant fishhook. Aside from the terrain, this gave the Union a strong defensive position. It also allowed Meade the ability to reinforce threatened sectors with his interior lines.

In contrast, the Confederates who were in parallel to the Union position had no option to reinforce with interior lines. They were also numerically inferior to the defending Union army.

General James Longstreet recommended leaving the battlefield where they could fight in a more favorable location. But Lee was flushed with the victory in the battle's first day and did not want to dampen his army's high morale. He believed that his army's fighting spirit would carry the day as it usually did.

George Meade

George Meade was appointed commander of the Army of the Potomac just three days before the Battle of Gettysburg. He arrived in the early hours of July 2, missing the entire first day of the battle.

The absence of Meade and for most of the day, Lee showed that the battle was spontaneous.

Meade showed excellent and calm leadership throughout the three-day battle. But politics and intrigue would haunt him after the battle as other people tried to vilify him and claim credit for the victory.

J. E. B. Stuart Missing

Lee ordered general J. E. B. Stuart to take three cavalry brigades and scout the Army of the Potomac. But he was caught up in skirmishes with small units of Union Cavalry from Delaware and New York. This delay meant Stuart failed to link with Ewell's army as planned.

By the time he linked up with Lee, he was too late to fight or provide reconnaissance.

Dan Sickles

Without orders, Union General Daniel Sickles advanced to

the Peach Orchard where he thought he could better use his artillery. But this left him vulnerable as he created a bulge in the Union lines. When he realized his mistake, he offered to go back to his original position but Meade said no as his retreating and reforming troops would be even more vulnerable.

Sickles' actions forced Meade to send 20,000 men as reinforcements.

The Union's line held, but Sickles' III Corps was virtually wiped out. Later, Sickles would claim that his actions won the battle.

Little Round Top

Little Round Top was at the Union's left flank. Capturing it would expose the Union to enfilading fire.

General Evander Law assaulted the position with units from Alabama and Texas. Facing them were Union Colonel Strong Vincent with units from Michigan, New York, Pennsylvania, and Maine.

The Confederate attacked several times during the battle.

In one of the war's most famous moments, Colonel Joshua Chamberlain, aware that they could not survive another attack, ordered a bayonet charge.

This charge startled the attackers and saved the Union's extreme left flank.

Ewell Attacks Cemetery Hill

After considering taking the hill as not practicable the day before, General Ewell finally attacked Cemetery Hill at dusk on Day two of the battle. His forces under General Jubal Early temporarily took the hill, but were pushed back by reinforcements, again via interior lines.

Pickett's Charge

The night before, General Meade correctly predicted that Lee's main attack the following day would be against his center. He prepared his defenses accordingly.

On the Confederate side, General Longstreet implored General Lee not to launch the attack, reasoning that they needed at least double the 12,500* men in the assault. The army also needed to cross about three quarters of a mile of open field, where they were vulnerable to artillery.

Before the charge, Lee and Meade engaged in an artillery barrage, at the time in the Western Hemisphere.

As the rebels charged, they were met with artillery. First by shell and solid shot. When the Confederates moved closer, they were met with cannister shots, and finally musket fire.

The Confederates suffered over 8,000 casualties during the assault. When Pickett had returned to the Confederacy lines and was later ordered by Lee to organize his division for defense, Pickett famously replied, "General, I have no division."

The "high-water mark" of the Confederacy refers to an area on Cemetery Ridge marking the farthest point reached by Confederate forces during Pickett's Charge.

Other sources say 15,000 men were part of the charge.

Gettysburg Address

The Gettysburg address was a 271-word speech delivered by President Lincoln on November 19,1863. It is one of the most famous speeches in history and began with the words, "Four scores and seven years ago…"

VICKSBURG CAMPAIGN

The Vicksburg campaign was a series of maneuvers to dislodge the Confederacy from their last controlled section of the Mississippi River.

Gibraltar of the Confederacy

Confederate President Jefferson Davis called Vicksburg "the nail that held the South's two halves together." Lincoln called it the "key to the war."

With most of the South's port blockaded as part of the Anaconda plan, Vicksburg became a critical part of the Confederacy's survival.

The fort at Vicksburg allowed resources like weapons, beef, molasses and others to flow freely between the Confederacy's two halves. Vicksburg stood on a high bluff overlooking a river bend. This terrain favored the defenders, and along with the fort's 172 guns and the nearby Port Hudson, both Union Army and Navy faced almost insurmountable challenges in any attack.

In the summer of 1862, the fort could've been captured easily but by fall, Pemberton had strengthened the defenses.

Riverboat Fleet

By late 1861, the Union had built a riverboat fleet composed of ironclad, timber-clad, and smaller steamers. This fleet was critical in the victories at both Fort Henry and Donelson.

By late 1862, this fleet had been vastly improved and was ready for Vicksburg.

Union In-fighting

General Halleck assigned Grant to launch a campaign against Vicksburg. Another general-politician, however, lobbied for the forming of another army to launch another campaign. General John McClernand's army was eventually split into two, one under him and another under William Sherman, both of them under Grant. This didn't sit well with the insubordinate McClernand who fought well, but continued undermining Grant.

During the siege, Grant finally fired McClernand for his unauthorized communication with the press.

Canals

Grant ordered the building of several canals, one after the other to bypass Vicksburg's defenses.

The army built canals on the De Soto peninsula, Lake Providence, and Duckport but all of these failed.

Grant Crosses the Mississippi

Grant launched two diversionary attacks to keep Pemberton guessing where the main attack would be. A cavalry charge in Mississippi and Sherman's feint north of the fort kept Pemberton busy and left some river crossings unguarded.

After an unsuccessful attack on the defenses at Grand Gulf along the Mississippi, Porter sent his ships as a protecting screen for the Union infantry in transport vessels.

Grant landed 17,000 soldiers, the largest amphibious operation in American military history until the invasion of Normandy.

For the next two weeks, Grant's army would get bigger and fight five battles.

Port Gibson

8,000 Confederates defended Port Gibson against 23,000 Union soldiers. This battle resulted in the capture of Grand Gulf, which became Grant's major supply port.

Miscommunication

Grant's strategy of cutting telegraph lines and destroying railroads disrupted the South's communication, especially the one between Pemberton and General Johnston who arrived to help him. Johnston's critical messages didn't arrive until days later, leaving Pemberton to guess whether they remained valid.

After Pemberton's defeat at Champion's Hill, he retreated and expected General William Loring's 8,000-strong army to join him. But Loring moved towards Jackson instead of Vicksburg.

By the time Pemberton retreated to the fort, he had lost over one-fourth of his army.

Siege

After several frontal attacks failed, Grant placed Vicksburg under siege. Day and night, Grant's artillery and Porter's fleet bombarded the city.

After holding out for forty-two days, and with supplies running out, Pemberton surrendered on July 4, 1863.

And with the fall of Port Hudson days later, the Union's control of the Mississippi was complete. The South's two halves were now separate.

EMANCIPATION PROCLAMATION

President Lincoln issued the Emancipation Proclamation on January 1,1863.

This meant that slaves who escaped from their masters and reached Union lines were now permanently free. Likewise, slaves in territories controlled by the Union Army were also free.

Escaped slaves held in the union as "contrabands" were also set free.

Proclamation

Lincoln wanted to issue the proclamation even earlier, but was advised to wait for a victory before the announcement.

After the Union's victory at Antietam, Lincoln issued the proclamation.

Initial Effects

There was joy among many African-Americans, both slaves and free at the proclamation.

In the South, there was outrage with many stating that the rebellion was justified as Lincoln sought to end slavery. Prices of slaves also grew higher.

African-Americans in the Union Army

During the Civil War, 180,000 African-Americans served in the Union army. About half were former slaves.

In the beginning, African-Americans were paid lower than

their white counterparts, until June 1864 when Federal Congress approved equal pay for all soldiers, regardless of race.

Effect Overseas

Support for the South from other countries mainly disappeared after the proclamation. Most developed countries had already abolished slavery and could not publicly support the South.

The Union's aim of eradicating slavery meant a country that supported the South also supported slavery. This ended any of the Confederacy's hopes of gaining official recognition.

Thirteenth Amendment

There was a fear among abolitionists that the war's end would invalidate emancipation. To ensure its lasting implementation, Lincoln and his legislative allies pushed for the Amendment, banning slavery and involuntary servitude except as a punishment for a crime.

This passed the House on January 31, 1865 and the Senate on April 8, 1965.

1864 ELECTIONS

The 1864 elections were held during an ongoing war, similar to the elections of 1812.

Expected Defeat

In early 1864, Lincoln expected defeat. The Union, despite its massive superiority in resources had not defeated the South. The South's major capitals remained in Confederate hands and the Southern Armies remained formidable.

There was also a growing peace movement.

Lincoln's Opponent

Lincoln's opponent was George McClellan, former Commander of the Army of the Potomac. He won the Democratic nomination over Thomas Seymour, former governor of Connecticut.

His running mate was George Pendleton who served both Senate and the House representing Ohio.

Lincoln's Ticket

For his running mate, Lincoln chose Andrew Johnson, former military governor of Tennessee.

The Fall of Atlanta

The fall of Atlanta meant that a Union military victory was inevitable.

Some historians have said that aside from Lincoln himself, only Union General William Sherman did more to ensure Lincoln's re-election.

Results

Lincoln won 55% of the popular vote compared to McClellan's 45%. He also won 212 electoral votes compared to McClellan's 21.

EUROPE'S ATTITUDE TOWARD THE CIVIL WAR

Some major leaders like France's Napoleon III sympathized with the Confederate's cause, but the international community was officially neutral throughout the war.

Lincoln repeatedly warned that any recognition of the Confederacy was tantamount to a declaration of war. While England depended on Southern cotton, a war with America would cut off other vital shipments from America including 40% of its wheat. It could also cause an invasion of Canada. By 1862, trade between England the Confederacy had fallen 90% from pre-war levels.

UNITED KINGDOM

Trent Affair

The American warship USS San Jacinto took control of the British mail steamer RMS Trent.

The Americans were informed that two Confederates acting as diplomats were on board the ship. Union Captain Charles Wilkes arrested James Mason and John Slidell of the Confederacy and removed them from the ship.

The British protested and began preparations for war, including sending 11,000 troops to Canada and preparing to blockade New York if needed. But these were mainly saber rattling. England and the United States had deep trade ties— England provided saltpeter while the US exported wheat. Banks in London also financed the railroad industry in the US. War meant defaulting on these loans.

In the end, the United States issued a statement that was accepted as an apology.

Lyons–Seward Treaty of 1862

This treaty between the United States and Great Britain was signed as an aggressive measure to end the Atlantic slave trade.

Among the provisions was the agreement that they would use their navies to seize merchant vessels carrying captured Africans, including vessels that bore indications of being a slave ship.

The large-scale illegal transport of slaves from Africa to

America was effectively ended.

British Shipyards

Despite protests from the US, a British shipyard built two warships for the Confederacy including the CSS Alabama, a screw sloop-of-war. CSS Alabama became a notorious commerce raider, attacking Union ships during the war. After the war, an international tribunal paid the US $15.5 million for damages caused by the British-built warships.

Another issue was Britain building ships that worked as blockade-runners for the South.

FRANCE

France was officially neutral throughout the war, but because of its interests in Mexico, toyed with the idea of supporting the Confederacy.

France, however, didn't want to risk war with the US without British support. Only Britain's refusal to join this position stopped France from further pursuing it.

Unlike the British, however, the French stopped the sale of the ironclad CSS Stonewall prior to delivery.

TRIVIA AND LITTLE-KNOWN FACTS

- Robert Lee had a son named Custis E. Lee. Unlike his father, Custis Lee finished first in his class at WestPoint.
- General George Thomas had a horse named Billy, named after Union General Sherman.
- John Pemberton resigned his commission as General after the fall of Vicksburg. Three days later, he accepted an offer to be a Lieutenant Colonel in an artillery unit.
- An early machine gun was invented during the Civil War. Richard Gatling invented the Gatling gun in 1861. Its design has survived to the modern day as the rotary cannon.
- There was an active semi-military organization active in the Midwestern states during the Civil War. The Knights of the Golden Circle aimed to annex all of Mexico, Cuba, and other territories and then merge them with the Southern States, forming a new country.
- A woman disguised herself as a man to fight in the Civil War. Sarah Edmonds disguised herself as Franklin Thompson and joined the 2nd Michigan Infantry Regiment. She fought in the First Battle of Bull Run and the Peninsular campaign in 1862.
- A confederate general wrote the popular infantry manual used by both the North and the South during the Civil War. William J. Hardee was a Confederate general who graduated from West Point in 1838. In 1855, he wrote the popular "Rifle and Light Infantry Tactics" in

1855.

- Richmond, Virginia is the best-known capital of the Confederacy. However, it was not the first. The honor belonged to Montgomery, Alabama just before the start of the Civil War.

- The Union had an aerial reconnaissance unit during the Civil War. The Balloon Corps was active until 1863.

- The first African American to receive the Medal of Honor was William H. Carney. Born into slavery, he was later freed and joined the 54th Massachusetts. Despite being badly wounded, he planted the flag in the sand, refusing to let it touch the ground even once. His actions rallied the troops.

- The Battle of Five Forks, one of the final major engagements of the war, is called the Waterloo of the Confederacy. It triggered the evacuation of Richmond, the Confederate's capital and led to Lee's surrender at Appomattox eight days later.

- During the Civil War, generals were 50% more likely to die compared to privates.

- Approximately 2.5% of the American population died during the Civil War. If 2.5% of the population died in war today, over eight million people would be dead.

- 2,100,000 men were mobilized for the Union compared to 880,000 for the South.

- The Battle of Gettysburg lasted 3 days. By the end of the second day, it was already the bloodiest battle of the war with 37,000 casualties.

- CSS Stonewall was an ironclad originally built for the Confederacy by France and was later sold to Japan. It became the Kōtetsu and played a key role in another Civil War –Japan's the Boishin War.